Presented

Megan, Mike, Eli, Leela, ~~Louis~~

From:

♡♡ Love, Maka & PaPa

Date:

April 11, 2022

Happy Easter

HONOR HB BOOKS

Inspiration and Motivation for the Seasons of Life

COOK COMMUNICATIONS MINISTRIES
Colorado Springs, Colorado • Paris, Ontario
KINGSWAY COMMUNICATIONS LTD
Eastbourne, England

Honor® is an imprint of
Cook Communications Ministries, Colorado Springs, CO 80918
Cook Communications, Paris, Ontario
Kingsway Communications, Eastbourne, England

HAPPY EASTER
© 2003, 2006 by Honor Books

Manuscript compiled by Lisa Hughes
Cover and Interior Design: BMB Design

First Printing, 2006
Printed in the United States of America

1 2 3 4 5 6 7 8 9 10 Printing/Year 10 09 08 07 06

ISBN 1-56292-747-7

Introduction

Easter is much more than just a day—it's a season that celebrates life, hope, and new beginnings. The Easter season tells a story—the story of the Savior's death, his glorious resurrection, and our hope for transformed lives.

Feel the excitement of the Easter season as you turn the pages of this book. The quotes, Scriptures, poetry, and traditions will inspire you, touch your heart, and make you smile. We have included a read-along story for children at the end for your family to share.

Happy Easter!

May Easter Day
To thy heart say,
"Christ died and rose for thee."
May Easter night
On thy heart write,
"O Christ, I live to *thee*."
—Anonymous

Easter Tradition

The custom of wearing new clothes on Easter Sunday can be traced back to AD 300 when Constantine, the first Christian emperor, decreed that the members of his court should wear their finest clothes on Easter as a sign of the importance of the occasion.

Ye happy bells of Easter Day!
Ring! Ring! Your joy
Thro' earth and sky;
Ye ring a glorious word.
The notes that swell in gladness tell
The rising of the *Lord!*

Did You Know?

The Dutch brought the traditions of the Easter egg and the Easter rabbit to America when they settled in Pennsylvania in the 1700s. The Dutch children used hats, bonnets, or fancy paper to prepare nests for the "Oschter Haws" (Easter rabbit). Over the years the hats were replaced by elaborate Easter baskets. The children believed that if they had been good, the Easter rabbit would come on Easter Eve and lay colorful eggs in their nests.

*W*elcome, happy morning! Age to age shall say:
Hell today is vanquished; Heaven is won today.
Lo! the Dead is living, God for evermore;
Him their true Creator, all his works adore.
—Venantius Fortunatus

O death, where is thy sting?
O grave, where is thy victory?
1 Corinthians 15:55 KJV

Easter says you can put truth in a grave,

But it won't stay there.

—Clarence W. Hull

Did You Know?

On March 27, 1513, the Spanish explorer Juan Ponce de Léon discovered the peninsula of Florida while he searched for the legendary Fountain of Youth. He named the land Florida because he made his discovery on Easter Sunday, and the Easter season was called Pascua Florida (Flowery Easter) in native Spain.

Did You Know?

A Dutch navigator named Jakob Roggeven discovered an island in the South Pacific on Easter Sunday, 1722; he named it Easter Island. It is approximately twenty-two hundred miles off the western coast of Chile, and numerous carvings made from soft volcanic stone are located there. These statues of gigantic heads are ten to forty feet high and weigh up to fifty tons.

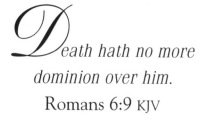

*Death hath no more
dominion over him.*
Romans 6:9 KJV

Tomb, thou shalt not hold him longer;
Death is strong, but Life is stronger;
Stronger than the dark, the light;
Stronger than the wrong, the right;
Faith and Hope triumphant say
Christ will rise on Easter Day.
—Phillips Brooks

Did You Know?

In the 1800s, Mrs. Thomas P. Sargent of Philadelphia discovered the white trumpet lilies in Bermuda. She brought the bulbs back to the United States; and this Bermuda lily soon became known as the Easter lily—the favored flower for decoration at Easter time.

Easter Activities

To create an Easter flower bouquet, place a glass upside down on a piece of colored tissue paper, draw around the rim, and cut out the circles. Stack three circles on top of each other—flower petals. Shape the petals by cutting curves around the edges. Insert a pin in the middle of the three petals. Hold the pin against a piece of thick craft wire—flower stem. Use different colored tissue paper, different size cups, and different designs to create a variety of flowers.

Did You Know?

The Easter basket did not become popular until the late 1800s, when candy became more common, thanks to a growing number of small candy manufacturers.

Did You Know?

In 1933, Paul H. King originated the idea of selling Easter seals as a fund-raising device for the International Society for Crippled Children. He believed the rehabilitation of crippled children that led to fuller lives and more activities for them harmonized with the meaning of Easter—Resurrection and New Life.

Snowdrop, lift your timid head,
All the earth is waking,
Field and forest, brown and dead,
Into life are breaking;
Snowdrops, rise and tell the story
How he rose, the Lord of *glory*.

Lilies! Lilies! Easter calls,
Rise to meet the dawning
Of the blessed light that falls
Thro' the Easter morning;
Ring your bells and tell the story,
How he rose, the Lord of *glory*.

Did You Know?

The Easter bonnet began as a wreath of flowers or leaves, with the circle symbolizing the roundness of the sun.

$\mathcal{J}$esus said to her,
"I am the resurrection and the life.
He who believes in me
will live, even though he dies;
and whoever lives and
believes in me will never die."
John 11:25–26

Easter Activities

To make hollow eggs, use eggs that have been kept at room temperature for several hours. Shake the eggs to break up the yolks. Using a needle, make a hole in the bigger end and move the needle back and forth to make the hole a little larger. Use the same needle to make a smaller hole in the small end of the egg. Place your lips over the second hole and blow the egg out through the larger hole and into a bowl. Clean the shell and stand it up to dry. Use the egg yolk and whites to make omelets or cakes. Color and decorate your hollow eggs with paint, markers, feathers, sequins, and beads.

Easter Bunny Cupcakes

One cupcake mix
White frosting
Shredded coconut

Large marshmallows
Cloves

Use your favorite cupcake recipe. Once baked, invert the cupcakes onto a platter. Spread white frosting on them; then sprinkle with shredded coconut. Use a large marshmallow to create the head and a half of a marshmallow for the tail. Use pieces of a large marshmallow and shape them into the two ears. Insert whole cloves or halves of black jelly beans for the eyes, one red hot for the mouth, and strands of coconut for the whiskers.

Easter Ice-cream Bunny

To make an ice-cream bunny, use firm vanilla ice cream and make a large scoop for the body of the bunny and a smaller scoop for the head. Set the two scoops on top of each other. Place about five miniature marshmallows on a toothpick. Make two of these and place them on the small scoop of ice cream to create the rabbit's ears. Decorate with red hots or jelly beans for the eyes and marshmallows for the mouth and tail. Place in the freezer until ready to serve.

In the bonds of death He lay
Who for our offence was slain;
But the Lord is risen today,
Wherefore let us all rejoice.
Singing loud, with cheerful voice,
Hallelujah!
—Martin Luther

Easter Activities

To create simple Easter Place Cards, begin by folding white cardstock paper in half. Use markers to draw grass on the bottom of one side of the card. Above the grass, write the guest's name. Around the name draw and color Easter rabbits. Glue cotton balls in place for the bunny tails.

If Easter means anything to modern man it means that eternal truth is eternal. You may nail it to the tree, wrap it up in grave clothes, and seal it in a tomb; but "truth crushed to earth, shall rise again."

—Donald Harvey Tippet

[Jesus] then began to teach them that the Son of Man must suffer many things and be rejected by the elders, chief priests and teachers of the law, and that he must be killed and after three days rise again.

Mark 8:31

Easter says to us that despite everything
to the contrary, his will for us will prevail, love will
prevail over hate, justice over injustice and oppression,
peace over exploitation and bitterness.
—Desmond Tutu

Did You Know?

The custom of coloring eggs at Easter seems to be a very old one. In 1290, King Edward I of England purchased 450 eggs that were to be colored or covered with leaf gold and given to the Royal Household.

Did You Know?

Originally, onionskins boiled in water were used to color eggs a light yellow. Then the eggs were boiled with flowers, logwood chips, or leaves to create other colors. Spinach leaves or anemone petals were used to create green, logwood chips for purple, gorse blossom or hickory bark for yellow, cochineal or madder root for red, and coffee or walnut shells for brown. An egg dyed red traditionally symbolized the blood of Christ. Today, vegetable dyes are used to create many brilliant colors.

The best news the world ever had came from a graveyard.

"He is not here, but is risen."

Luke 24:6 KJV

"Christ the Lord is risen today,"

Sons of men and angels say.

Raise your joys and triumphs high;

Sing, ye heavens, and earth reply.

—Charles Wesley

Lift your voices in
triumph on high,
For Jesus is risen and
man cannot die.

—Henry Ward

The God of our fathers raised Jesus from the dead—whom you had killed by hanging him on a tree. God exalted him to his own right had as Prince and Savior that he might give repentance and forgiveness of sins to Israel.

Acts 5:30–31

Easter Traditions

The Pennsylvania Dutch were well known for an Easter decoration called the Easter egg bird. This was a decorated eggshell in which four holes were made to insert a handcrafted head, wings, and tail of a bird. Another opening was made on the shell so that the bird could be attached to a piece of thread and displayed in the home.

Easter Traditions

In Pennsylvania in the nineteenth century, it was customary for men and children to engage in egg-eating contests. On Easter Sunday and Monday, they also played a game called "picking eggs" that was designed to test the strength of eggshells by hitting the ends of eggs together. The broken egg was awarded as a prize to the person whose egg remained whole.

Our Lord has written the promise of
resurrection, not in books alone,
but in every leaf in springtime.
—Martin Luther

Easter is a day to fan the ashes of dead hope,
a day to banish doubts and seek the slopes where the
sun is rising, to revel in the faith which transports
us out of ourselves and the dead past into
the vast and inviting unknown.

—*Lewiston Tribune* [Idaho]

Did You Know?

One legend states that Simon of Cyrene, who carried Christ's cross for him, was actually an egg peddler. When he returned to his basket of eggs after his somber walk with the cross, he found all the eggs in his basket beautifully decorated.

Easter in Other Countries

The people of Mexico create cascarones for Easter. These are blown-out eggs filled with confetti and then the holes are sealed with brightly colored tissue-paper "hats." They are then cracked on people's heads. Some people say that the cracked egg symbolizes Christ breaking out of his tomb.

Come, ye saint, look here and wonder,
See the place where Jesus lay;
He has burst his bands asunder;
He has borne our sins away;
Joyful tidings.
Yes, the Lord has risen today.
—Thomas Kelly

This Jesus God raised up, and of that all of us are witnesses.

Acts 2:32 NRSV

Did You Know?

The first White House Easter Egg Roll was held on Easter Monday in 1878. President Rutherford B. Hayes and First Lady Lucy Hayes hosted the event, which took place on the South Lawn.

Easter Traditions

Egg rolling was another popular sport that is still practiced today in some parts of the world. People roll colored, hard-boiled eggs down a hill to see whose egg can remain unbroken for as long as possible.

'Twas a thief that said the
last kind word to Christ:
Christ took the kindness
and forgave the theft.
—Robert Browning

[The criminal said,] "We are punished justly, for we are getting what our deeds deserve. But this man has done nothing wrong." Then he said, "Jesus, remember me when you come into your kingdom." Jesus answered him, "I tell you the truth, today you will be with me in paradise."

Luke 23:41–43

Easter Traditions

Following World War II, an annual Easter Egg Rolling Contest was held in New York's Central Park. Children, aged five to twelve, used wooden spoons to roll wooden eggs along an established lane. The winners received toys and other gifts.

Easter Activities

The German Egg Blowing Game is played by placing a blown egg in the center of a table, where guests have been seated. One person blows the egg across the table to the other side. The person who is closest to the egg responds by blowing it back. No one is allowed to touch the egg, and anyone who lets the egg fall off the table is automatically out of the game. The last person at the table is the winner.

O chime of sweet Saint Charity,
Peal soon that Easter morn
When Christ for all shall risen be,
And in all hearts new-born!
—James Russel Lowell

"I, when I am lifted up from the earth, will draw
all men to myself."
John 12:32

Did You Know?

South Africa is the home of the largest Easter Egg ever made. The egg was made entirely of marshmallow and chocolate. It weighed 4,068 kilos and was 7.65 meters high.

Did You Know?

On March 20, 1999, the world's largest Easter-egg hunt was held in Victoria, Australia, as a means to raise funds for the Vision Australia Foundation. Army troops hid about one hundred fifty thousand chocolate Easter eggs that were provided by Cadbury's. Approximately three thousand children participated in this event that was coordinated by companies all over Australia.

They took palm branches and
went out to meet him, shouting,

"Hosanna!"

"Blessed is he who comes in the name of the Lord!"

"Blessed is the King of Israel!"

John 12:13

He will swallow up death in victory;
and the Lord GOD will wipe away
tears from off all faces.

Isaiah 25:8 KJV

Did You Know?

The most ornate Easter eggs are actually not eggs at all. Rather, they are called Fabergé eggs and were created over one hundred years ago by a jeweler named Carl Fabergé in Russia. He handcrafted these elaborate eggs out of gold, silver, and jewels. When opened, each egg usually displays a hidden treasure, such as tiny figures of people, animals, or buildings. At Easter time, the Russian tsar would give these exquisite eggs to his friends and family.

Lenten Season

Shrovetide

Shrovetide or Carnival is the name for the last three or four days before Ash Wednesday and the beginning of Lent. All the days in Shrovetide have special names and customs associated with them, including Egg Saturday, Quinquagesima Sunday, Collop Monday, and Shrove Tuesday.

Egg Saturday

The Saturday before Ash Wednesday was once called
Egg Saturday because children traveled to various houses
and begged for eggs. The eggs they received were to be
eaten before the beginning of Lent. If they were not
given any eggs at a particular home, they threw
broken dishes at the front door.

Collop Monday

The Monday of Shrovetide was once called Collop Monday. Collop is an old English word that means a cut of cured meat. All bacon, eggs, and fried collops of meat were supposed to be consumed by Collop Monday so that none would be left when Lent began.

Shrove Tuesday

In England as well as other countries, the day before Ash Wednesday is still known as Shrove Tuesday, Pancake Tuesday, Guttit Tuesday, or Goodish Day—due to the number of good things eaten then. It was customary to make pancakes on this day because the cooking fat, butter, and eggs used in the preparation had to be consumed prior to the beginning of Lent.

Did You Know?

After the Reformation, the church bell that had once been used to call Christians to confession during Shrovetide became known as the Pancake Bell—the signal for pancakes to be made and for the sports, games, and other festivities to begin.

Fat Tuesday

In Sweden, Shrove Tuesday is known as Fat Tuesday. On this day the people eat semlas, or Fat Tuesday buns, which are big buns made out of wheat flour and filled with almond paste and whipped cream. The buns are served in bowls of hot milk. In Iceland, these semlas are called "cream buns," and Fat Tuesday is called Bursting Day because everyone eats an excessive amount of food.

Lent Traditions

In various parts of England, egg shackling is a popular game played on Shrove Tuesday. To play this game, children write their names on eggs and bring them to school. The eggs are then placed in a sieve and shaken until only one is left whole. The child whose egg is unbroken receives a cash prize, and the cracked eggs are either sent to a local hospital or returned home to make pancakes.

Lent Traditions

In 1950, housewives in Liberal, Kansas, U.S.A., challenged the housewives in Olney, Buckinghamshire, England, to a pancake race on Shrove Tuesday. The British housewives readily accepted the challenge, and since then, the International Pancake Day Race has become an annual event. Courses of identical distance are set up in each location, and the times of each of the winners are compared by telephone.

Ash Wednesday

The first day of Lent was formerly referred to as the "Beginning of the Fast." However, in A.D. 1099, Pope Urban II introduced the name Ash Wednesday. On this day, many Christians participated in a ceremony where blessed ashes were placed on their foreheads in the form of a cross. Then, a priest said, "Remember, man, that thou art dust, and to dust thou shalt return."

Did You Know?

Many years ago, most Christians did not eat meat, cheese, butter, cooking fats, or eggs during Lent—a period of forty days. Today, Christians often give up something they enjoy, like candy or ice cream. In addition to being a period of fasting, Lent was also designed to be a time of mourning. People were expected to give up various entertainments and festivities. The atmosphere at the church reflected this state of mourning: There were no floral decorations or organ music. In many countries the women dressed in black and wore no jewelry.

Lent Traditions

To help count down the days of Lent, many Greeks cut out a paper figure of a nun. She did not have a mouth, since fasting was a crucial part of Lent; her hands were crossed in prayer; and she had seven feet, one for each of the seven weeks of Lent. One of the feet was torn off at the end of each week. Another method used in Greece was sticking seven feathers into an onion or a potato. This was hung from the ceiling and used in a similar fashion.

Lent Traditions

In the United States and Great Britain, hot cross buns are a popular food during Easter. These sweet rolls are stuffed with raisins and candied fruit; then sugar frosting is used to form a cross on the top of the buns. Initially, these hot cross buns were baked and eaten only on Good Friday, but now they are baked all through the period of Lent.

Fourth Sunday of Lent

In Luxembourg, the fourth Sunday of Lent is called Bretzelsonndeg, which means Pretzel Sunday. On this day the boys present to their girlfriends decorated cakes that look like pretzels. If the girl admires her suitor, she responds on Easter Sunday by offering him a hollow decorated egg filled with bonbons and by walking with him to the park. On leap year, the tradition is reversed: The girl gives the pretzel cake and the boy gives the Easter egg.

Fourth Sunday of Lent

The fourth Sunday in Lent is called Mid-Lent Sunday or Mothering Sunday in England. Children return to their mothers' homes to visit them and bring them flowers, simnel cakes, and other gifts to celebrate this day.

Did You Know?

Mothering Sunday never became an established custom in the United States. However, in 1907, Anna Jarvis, of Philadelphia, decided that there should be one day in the year when children honored their mothers. She organized a special service to be held in a local church, and she asked attendees to wear white carnations. The service was a huge success. In 1914, largely due to her efforts, Congress determined the second Sunday in May to be Mother's Day.

Easter Traditions

It was customary for young men to send gloves to their girlfriends on Easter Eve. If the girlfriend accepted the gloves and wore them to church on Easter Sunday, it meant that courtship was progressing very well and would probably result in marriage.

Easter Traditions

In Russia on Easter weekend, young women are given Easter charms shaped like eggs. The eggs are usually made of semiprecious stones, like quartz and jade. The charms are placed on a necklace, and a girl's popularity is judged by the number of charms she receives.

God forbid that I should
glory, save in the cross of
our Lord Jesus Christ.
Galatians 6:14 KJV

Teach me, my God, to bear my cross
As thine was borne;
Teach me to make of every loss
A crown of thorn.
—John Keble

Every noble crown is, and
On earth will forever be,
a crown of thorns.
—Thomas Carlisle

"Easter"

The air is like a butterfly
With frail blue wings.
The happy earth looks at the sky
And sings.
—Joyce Kilmer

Easter in Other Countries

In Switzerland, tiny flowers, leaves, and other decorations are attached to the eggs prior to boiling them in an onion peel. This technique results in an elaborate white pattern on a tinted background. Sometimes a design or message is traced on an already dyed egg with a white wax pencil; other times a knife is used to scratch off some of the dye and to create an elaborate white design.

Easter in Other Countries

The Easter eggs in Hungary are generally white and decorated with a red flower pattern. The pattern is first traced on with wax; then the eggs are covered with cold paint. They usually contain a message, Scripture verse, or picture of a man and woman in costume. The children exchange their eggs with one another as expressions of friendship. In some parts of the country, the eggs are hung on little Easter trees that young men place outside the homes of the girls they wish to court.

Come, ye saints, look here and wonder,
See the place where Jesus lay;
He has burst his band asunder;
He has borne our sins away;
Joyful tidings,
Yes, the Lord has risen today.
—Thomas Kelly

If you confess with your mouth, "Jesus is Lord," and believe in your heart that God raised him from the dead, you will be *saved*.

Romans 10:9

Easter Traditions

The people in Poland and the Ukraine call their Easter eggs pysanki, which means "written eggs." A needle or small metal tube is used to draw designs or pictures on the eggs with wax. The designs are often geometrical or abstract patterns, and Christian symbols like the fish and the cross are also often used. Once the design is completed, the eggs are then dyed, and the wax is melted off. It often takes a person several days to create just one of these elaborate eggs.

All Christian worship is a witness of the resurrection of him who liveth for ever and ever. Because he lives, "now abideth faith, hope, charity."

—Lyman Abbott

Easter Traditions

Egg shackling was a popular game played at Easter time in
England and many European countries. Boys held
hard-boiled eggs in their right hands and attempted
to smash as many other eggs as possible while
keeping their own eggs whole.

Easter Traditions

The Pennsylvania Dutch introduced the tradition of an Easter egg tree. They used needles to poke holes in eggs; then they blew the contents out. The eggshells were painted and decorated, and loops of colorful ribbon were pasted on the eggs so that they could be placed tip downwards on an evergreen or leafless tree. The Easter tree was then placed on a table in the center of the room. It was decorated, not only with the painted eggs, but also with ornaments, sugar people, cake animals, pieces of chocolate, and candy. Underneath the tree, an Easter rabbit or lamb was placed on the table to watch over all of the gifts.

Christ has turned all our sunsets into dawns.

—Clement of Alexandria

Ride on, ride on in majesty!

In lowly pomp ride on to die:

Bow thy meek head to mortal pain:

Then take, O God, thy power and reign.

—Henry Hart Milman

Easter in Other Countries

In Scotland and northern England, a custom called "lifting" or "heaving" was popular on Easter Monday. A "chair" was made out of people's hands, and a person was tossed into the air three times and then kissed. The men "lifted" the women on Easter Monday, and the women "lifted" the men on Easter Tuesday. This custom was intended to represent Christ's resurrection.

Easter in Other Countries

In Popayán, Columbia, on the Tuesday before Easter, a ceremony called the Feast of the Prisoners takes place. The archbishop, various government officials, and other people form a procession to the prison, bringing with them an abundance of food. The prisoners are served as they listen to speeches. In a gesture representing the choosing of Barabbas, one of the prisoners is selected, presented with donations of food and money, and released from prison.

In vain with stone the cave they barred;

In vain the watch kept ward and guard;

Majestic from the spoiled tomb.

In pomp of triumph Christ is come.

—John Mason Neale

They found the stone rolled away from the tomb, but when they

entered, they did not find the body of the Lord Jesus.

Luke 24:2–3

The stone at the tomb of Jesus was a pebble to the Rock of Ages inside.

—Frederick Beck

Easter in Other Countries

During Holy Week in Champagne, France, it has been the custom since the thirteenth century to hold a jousting tournament. Before the jousting begins, the young men ride their horses through the town, carrying long lances. They also carry a large wooden sculpture of Jesus, which they place on a platform in front of the church.

"Easter Week"
Palm Sunday

Did You Know?

The majority of the palms used on Palm Sunday in the United States is harvested in Florida, whose state tree happens to be the cabbage palm. Thousands of acres of cattle land in this state are leased for the sole purpose of cutting the cabbage palm to use in church services on Palm Sunday.

Did You Know?

On the Saturday evening before Palm Sunday in Yugoslavia, it is customary for a young girl to place flower blossoms in a bowl of water. On Palm Sunday morning, she washes her face in the water because legend states it will make her beautiful.

The Sunday before Easter is called Palm Sunday, and it marks the beginning of Holy Week or the time of the passion of our Lord. On Palm Sunday, many churches pass out palm branches or tiny crosses made from palms in remembrance of Christ's triumphal entry into Jerusalem. People shouted for joy and waved palm branches before him as a gesture of respect and honor.

On Palm Sunday in the Black Forest in Germany, tall poles are decorated with pussy willows, cross drawing, foliage, and streamers. They are carried to the church for a blessing and then placed in the dooryards of homes. In many parts of Germany, a wooden image of a donkey—the animal that carried Jesus into Jerusalem for his triumphal entry—is carried into the church. The people then go forward to touch it and to receive a blessing.

In England, Palm Sunday was sometimes called Spanish Sunday, because children made a sweet drink from small pieces of Spanish licorice stirred into a bottle of water. The water used in this concoction had to come from a holy well, and a special pilgrimage was made to gather the water. The children circled the well three times, filled and shook their bottles, then merrily sipped their drinks.

"Easter Week"
Maundy Thursday

The Thursday before Easter is called Maundy Thursday. Maundy comes from a Latin word that means "a command," and it refers to when Jesus commanded his followers to love one another. On this special day many people, including world leaders, try to follow that command by giving maunds, or gifts, to the poor.

From a very early time in church history, it was tradition for priests and others to wash the feet of twelve or more poor people on Maundy Thursday in remembrance of Christ washing his apostles' feet on the night before his crucifixion. In later years, gifts of money, food, and clothes were presented in addition to the ceremonial foot washing.

On Holy Thursday in the Czech Republic, the people eat "Judases" for breakfast. These little cakes are made from twisted dough. They look like rope, representing the fate of Judas Iscariot who hanged himself in grief after he turned Jesus over to his enemies. The cakes are served with honey.

"*Easter Week*"
Good Friday

On Good Friday morning, Bermudians enjoy hot cross buns. Their Easter breakfast is called the "Codfish and Banana Breakfast." Boneless, skinless salt cod is boiled along with peeled whole potatoes. The dish is then served with either olive oil poured over the top or a scoop of mayonnaise. A portion of sliced bananas accompanies the fish.

On Good Friday in Bermuda, it is customary for children of all ages to fly kites. Various prizes are awarded to the children with the biggest, most beautiful, or longest-flown kites. This tradition can be traced back to a Bermudian Sunday school teacher who tried to explain Christ's ascension to heaven to his class.

For Christians, Good Friday is the most solemn day of the year. On this day, the passion and death of the Lord is remembered by church services of sorrow and thankfulness. In some parts of Europe, this day is called Holy or Great Friday.

The French refer to Easter as Pâques, which begins with a solemn commemoration on Good Friday. As a sign of their mourning for Jesus, the French do not ring their church bells from Good Friday to Easter Sunday.

For centuries it has been customary in England to play marbles on Good Friday. Some believe that it is linked to dice throwing that was practiced by Roman soldiers at the foot of the cross. Every year on Good Friday in Sussex, England, a marble championship is held; and the champions are awarded a silver cup.

On Good Friday at Ayot St. Peter in Herfordshire, England, they ring the Nine Tailors for Our Lord's death. Ringing the Nine Tailors (or tellers) is an old custom that is used to inform the townspeople when someone has died. The bell rings nine times if a man has died, six times for a woman, and three times for a child. Then, after a brief pause, the bell rings again to indicate the age of the dead person. So, on Good Friday at Ayot St. Peter, the bell rings nine times for Christ; then the bell rings another thirty-three times to mark his age.

There is an inn in London called the Widow's
Son, where each year on Good Friday a hot cross bun is
placed in a basket next to many others from previous years.
This tradition started in the early nineteenth century when
the owner of the inn set aside a bun on each Good Friday
in hopes that her sailor son, who was at sea,
would safely return.

"Easter Week"
Easter Eve

In years past on Easter Eve in certain parts of Germany, giant oak wheels with straw-packed spokes were placed on the top of a hill and set on fire. These wheels were sometimes up to seven feet in diameter and often weighed over eight hundred pounds. People watched as they rolled down the hill, and the field where the wheel came to rest was considered blessed for a rich harvest.

On Easter Eve in Lithuania, the people take two baskets to the church to be blessed. One basket contains small pieces of the food to be eaten for breakfast on Easter Sunday. The other basket holds bread and meat for the poor people who are waiting outside the church.

In some Irish villages, a cake dance took place on Easter Eve. The man declared the best dancer was awarded a large cake, which he shared with his dance partner as well as the rest of the guests. The expression "he takes the cake" was derived from this custom.

In Greece, the Resurrection service is often held at midnight on Easter Eve. The people carry white candles decorated with ribbons and flowers. The lights are out in the church when the service begins. The priest enters carrying a lighted candle, and he says, "Come ye, partake of the never-setting Light and glorify Christ, who is risen from the dead." The people light their candles from his candle; then they pass their light on to the person beside them until the entire church is filled with light.

"*Easter Week*"
Easter Sunday

From the time of the apostles, the early Christians observed a strict two-day fast from Good Friday until Easter Sunday, during which they did not eat or drink anything. Over time, a longer fasting period was introduced in preparation for Easter Sunday. During the third and fourth centuries, most churches gradually accepted the forty-day fasting period known as Lent. It begins on Ash Wednesday and ends on the Saturday before Easter Sunday.

Many scholars believe Christ's crucifixion occurred on Friday, April 17, in AD 30. If so, then Christ's resurrection took place on Sunday, April 19. For many years, however, people's opinions differed as to the actual date of the events, so in AD 325, at the Council of Nicea, a group of Christian leaders decided that Easter should always be celebrated on the Sunday following the first full moon—that is on or after the vernal equinox. Hence, the date of Easter Sunday varies from year to year. It may come as early as March 22 or as late as April 25.

It is believed that in 1609, the first sunrise service on Easter Sunday was held by a group of Spaniards exploring North America.

Cadillac Mountain in Maine is the location of the first Easter Sunday sunrise service in the United States because it is the easternmost pinnacle of the country. The last ceremony on the mainland of the United States takes place in Yosemite National Park.

A legend popular in Great Britain and Ireland said that the sun always danced when it was rising on Easter Sunday morning because it was so excited that Christ had risen from his tomb. People believed that they could see it dancing if they climbed up to the top of a hill, so they gathered on hilltops to watch the sun rise on Easter morning.

In Russia, Easter Sunday morning was filled with the sound of thousands of church bells ringing, for anyone who desired could go to the church and ring the bells. In the afternoon it was customary to visit friends; in fact, it was considered rude if you failed to visit every single one of your friends. The visitors always received the same greeting: "How kind of you! Come in! Christohs voskress [Christ is risen]!"

In Venezuela, an annual migration of freshwater turtles occurs every year around Easter. The turtles travel hundreds of miles to lay their eggs in the sand. The Venezuelans make jewelry from the turtle shells, and cakes from the turtle meat are served as delicacies at the Easter Sunday meal.

In Finland, the term for Easter comes from the verb päästä, which means to get free. On Easter Sunday, people "get free from" the Lenten fast. It also signifies the day Jesus was freed from his tomb. They make a special Easter dessert called mämmi made from rye-meal and malt. Other foods served at the Easter meal are eggs, milk, blood sausage, pies, lamb, cheese, and veal.

On Easter Sunday in Greece, it is customary to eat a special bread called the Bread of Christ. The top crust is marked with the Greek cross, which represents the crucifixion. The bread loaf is also decorated with Easter eggs.

The meal on Easter Sunday in Poland is arguably the most elaborate of all the feasts served in all the countries that celebrate Easter. The Polish Easter table is decorated with greenery and the ornately designed pysanki, or Easter eggs. Either a lamb made of sugar or a lamb-shaped cake serves as the centerpiece of the table.

In Portugal, Folar is a sweetbread served on Easter Sunday. It is baked in a flat, circular shape and decorated with hard-boiled eggs. The children give each other gifts of sugar-covered almonds that have been placed in small cornucopias made of colored paper.

On Easter Sunday in Tampa, Florida, thirty-three white pigeons are released, symbolizing the number of years Christ lived on earth.

In Russia, Poland, and other Eastern European countries, people greet each other on Easter Sunday by saying, "Christ is Risen!" The other person then responds, "He is risen indeed." They then usually exchange three kisses with each other. The Easter meal consists of the richest food the family can afford, and the priest blesses it before it is eaten.

In Europe, Easter Sunday is celebrated by lighting huge bonfires on hilltops and in churchyards. The bonfires are commonly called "Judas fires" because effigies of Judas Iscariot, the betrayer of Jesus, are often burned in the fires.

The Paschal or Easter Chronicle, a famous historical work written in AD 629 at Constantinople, recalls the events from the beginning of the world until that date. The book is named the Easter Chronicle because Christ's resurrection on the first Easter Sunday was deemed to be the most important event in history.

A Read-aloud Easter Story

Long ago in the land of Judea, an amazing man named Jesus walked through the countryside and went to the Temple for worship. Along with his disciples, Jesus preached about God's great love for all people. He told the people that he was God's Son—his only son. He said that he was the one sent by God—the Messiah, the Christ who would bring a sinful people back to God. He also healed the sick and performed many miracles. Soon crowds followed him everywhere he went.

The religious leaders in Jerusalem quickly became concerned as they heard of Jesus' growing popularity. One day, Jesus rode into Jerusalem on a donkey as crowds called him the King of kings and threw palm branches in his path.

On that very day, the religious leaders decided Jesus had to be stopped at all costs. Later that week, he was arrested. Liars said bad things about him and said he had to die. The next day, Jesus was crucified between two thieves. His enemies rejoiced. They felt they had silenced his voice forever.

Jesus' disciples and close friends were very sad. They could not believe that their great leader was dead. Carefully, they took his body down from the cross, wrapped it in grave cloth, and placed it in a tomb. Then they stood watching with tear-stained faces as Roman soldiers sealed the tomb with an enormous boulder and placed guards nearby.

That might have been the end of this story—a good and gentle man, lied about and sent to his death. But it was not! Three days after Jesus was crucified, a few of his followers went to the tomb and found the big rock rolled away. The body of Jesus was gone! They saw the grave cloth that had encircled his body lying undisturbed, and angels said Jeus had risen from the grave! Now it was Jesus' followers who rejoiced!

Throughout history, there have been many good and gentle men who have died for the message they preached. But, unlike Jesus, the stones that were placed over their graves continue to lock them in death. Only Jesus has risen! Only Jesus is the mighty, only begotten *Son of God!*

Additional copies of this
and other Honor products are available
wherever good books are sold.

If you have enjoyed this book,
or if it has had an impact on your life,
we would like to hear from you.

Please contact us at:

Honor Books
Cook Communications Ministries, Dept. 201
4050 Lee Vance View
Colorado Springs, CO 80918
Or visit our Web site: www.cookministries.com